A 40 Point Guide To Peeing In New York

By Ray Tempus

copyright © 2005

A 40 Point Guide To Peeing In New York

Copyright © 2003 By Ray Tempus

Published by
One Temptation Press
545 Eighth Ave. Suite #401
New York, New York 10018
onetpress@yahoo.com

All Rights Reserved. No part of this book may be reproduced or transmitted in any form or by any means, electronic or mechanical including photocopying, recording, or by any information storage and retrieval system, without written permission from the author or the publisher except for the inclusion of brief quotations in a review.

ISBN: 0-9772587-0-X
First Printing: 2005

Acknowledgments

If you think I'm crazy for doing this book, wanna hear something even crazier? I actually left a Wall Street career to pursue my desire to communicate my social views through art. Thus, painter/sculptor.

Allow me this space to thank my encouraging family and many instructors along the way. I also want to thank: Sherry, Jenna, Rodlyn, Chasmo Green & the Lady Lee, Robert and Christine D. for your support along the way.

As a painter, my communication isn't this descriptive, so it's fun to kind of run my mouth for a change.

Heartfelt thanks to Iris & Monique for creative input, as well as the technical expertise to make this project happen. Also the good people at the Village Copier for much assistance. And, of course, special thanks to Doug Ward at One Temptation Press for the hard work and commitment to publish this guide.

And above all, I laugh thank you's to the crazy ladies that participated in the interviews. My cute friend Katie for entries #14 & 15, Charitie for entry #38 and Demian's friend (whomever she may be), for entry #18.

Oh, . . . and Margarita. (wink)

Ray Tempus

New York City is unique in many ways. Most obvious is the landscape/cityscape. The absence of alleys, freestanding buildings, large trees, or streets void of pedestrians and the unavoidable need to walk long distances, makes "peeing" one of the biggest dilemmas people of the city face (visitors too).

  After being ticketed for this quality of life infraction one rainy Saturday evening, on a desolate street, under a drippy scaffold, I realized the need to refine a few incognito ways to perform this function in even less ideal situations.

  I believe men have more ways to do this, though I can't be sure. Some women's garments seem better suited to "peeing on the sly."

The female entries are based on actual interviews unless otherwise noted. Of those by observation, I won't include the horrible drunkard who just stopped walking, squatted and peed, asking as I passed, "what's a matter, you never seen a lady do the pee-pee?" Nor will I include my friend who somehow, while driving, fills a large container. I don't know if it happens while parked, or at a light. She never misses a word of the on-going conversation. I've witnessed this several times but I haven't a clue as to how it happens. Therefore it can't be included.

All male entries are first hand. Not included are those that lack good judgment. What remains, hopefully, will solve this dilemma for you and yours. This is a must read for visitors. This journal has been pocket sized for your convenience. Now go out there and pee freely!

Most entries include anti-splashing technique. Splash is the single biggest problem. It makes noise. But worse, it'll ruin your shoes. Makes them smell like pee, and the acid kind of rots them.

Oh, and about that ticketing incident. The judge threw it out for lack of evidence. How about that! A police van with half a dozen of New York's Finest witnessing this heinous act, and nobody thought to gather the evidence.

Question: How many New York City police officers does it take to scoop up pee-pee in the rain?

Answer: (See entry #20)

Proper foot spacing and positioning.

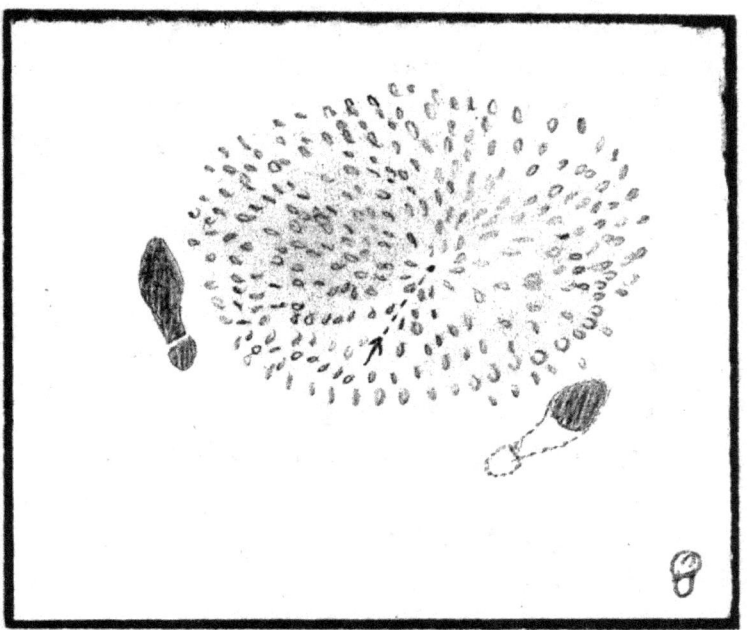

Square feet widely with toes pointed outward. Aim slightly to one side stepping back with the foot on that side rising onto the toe of the same foot. The idea is to keep splash off of your shoes.

~~Do's~~ and Don'ts

- Never go into what appears to be a dark corner then turn your back to pee. Though you think you're hiding, it's obvious that you are peeing, dummy. You must hide in plain view.
- Never pee into a hole near a tree. The holes are rat dens, they'll come out.
- Never pee into the river from the promenade. That's nasty.
- Never pee into a sidewalk grate near a subway station where you can see the train below. You'll pee on the people waiting for the train.

O.k., I know. I shouldn't have told some of you about this.

♀ #1 <u>Observation:</u> We've all done this one. Saturday night; 'THAT GIRL', you got some money cause ya' just got paid. A little aerobics before the shower gets the blood flowing and the gas out. You spray your underarms, eat altoids and dress your best, not missing a beat. Fine dining, wine and candlelight; romantic moonlight walk when suddenly...in a too hurried to be sexy voice cutie says, "Oh honey, I have to pee. Now! Stand in front of me and act natural. Hold my purse, and don't look."

    She then squats behind a car and pees. I don't know if it's the silly looking squat or the sound of splashing pee that kills the sparkle, but it's definitely gone. Hell, now you might as well fart.

♂ #2 Walk between two parked vehicles (preferably trucks), as though you are crossing. Turn and face the curb. The downward slope takes the splash away from you.

♂ #3 Duck into a deep unmanned doorway, face the street, and allow the pee to flow down the wall to eliminate splash. (20-30 seconds of pedestrian clearance required)

♂ #4 Faux use of a pay phone. Use only the ones with side cover and a slope on the supports. Duck in, hold the receiver and pee on to the side support to eliminate splash. This gives you cover on three sides. You can use your back for 360° coverage if necessary.

     P.S. Changing into the, 'Superman', costume isn't all, 'Clark Kent', used the phone booth for.

♂ #5 If no one is walking toward you, evening is sufficient cover. Walk close to the buildings aiming towards the wall. Pee on the buildings while walking. This technique eliminates splash.

♂ #6 If no one is behind you, stand beside a mailbox and stretch your arms upward as though you are exercising. Pee down the side of the mailbox. Splash is minimized, though not eliminated. Still, space your feet and point your toes outward.

♂ #7 Rain makes things easy. 20 seconds of overhead cover and hold your umbrella like a shield.

♂ #8 Rain can make for fewer pedestrians. Space your feet and pee while walking. The natural cohesiveness of water limits splash. Raincoats are good cover. Ask any masher.

♂ #9 Of course the few desolate streets are easy. (More of em' at night.) Just pee.

♂ #10 After dusk if people are in front of, but not behind you, turn around and pee while walking backward. Splash can be a problem even though you're walking away from the pee. You must quickly develop a technique for missing your shoes. Aiming at a wall is always an option.

♂ #11 When visiting or passing a park and no facilities are available (why do they keep them locked?)………Don't go behind a tree!

Too obvious!

Go to the grass and do a few pushups.

No visible wet spot.
No splash.
Better body.

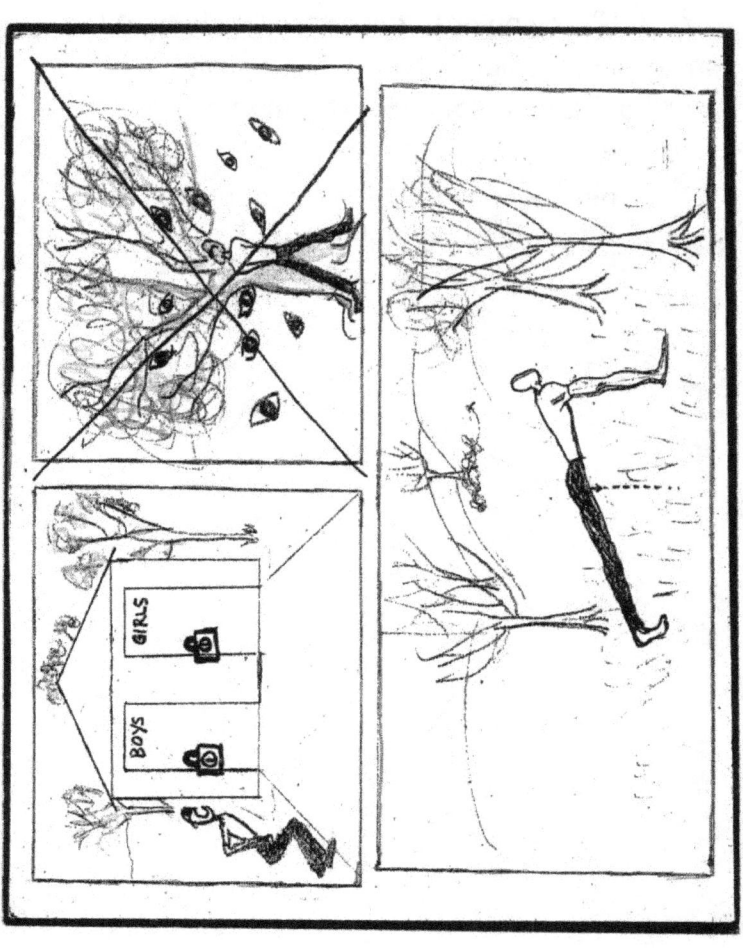

♂ #12 If you are too tired, too lazy, or otherwise unmotivated to do a push-up or two. Lie on your side facing no one and pee.

No spot, no splash, in a perfect position for reading or napping.

♀ #13 <u>Observation:</u> On occasions I've observed a lady squatting between cars while her friends act as cover. The cute one is always the one peeing. More complimentary drinks I guess. Even the advantages of beauty are temporarily neutralized by the ridiculous squat and the splashing sound of pee-pee.

♀ #14 <u>Interview:</u> the comeback of the miniskirt, coupled with the proliferation of the thong panty has, lessened the time and difficulties for women. While walking and peeing is still not an option, many other methods are do-able. A bus shelter seat, park bench, briefcase, or anything seat height.

With a little pedestrian clearance, sit half way on seat (one booty cheek), use a one finger light switch motion to shift the panty, and pee. Position feet to avoid splash.

♀ #15 <u>Interview:</u> (second entry, complete with pose). Same attire, cover of night. Place one foot on a thigh high surface. Step far away from surface with the other foot. Same one finger light switch motion to shift the thong, and pee. Splash can be a problem here. Step wide.

♂ #16 Pretending to pick through the trash, while degrading (especially if you're well dressed), offers ample cover. Pee while faux picking. The cardboard boxes and plastic bags soften the pee splash. And Hey, you could get lucky! One man's trash is another man's treasure.

Thing is, people think (and correctly so), that it's rude to watch a trash picker.

♀ #17 Car ownership provides many opportunities. We'll just use the easiest one. Open the door, stand in the "V" and pee. Splash is a problem here. Cups are not allowed in this journal, as peeing into ones own hand is nasty.

♀ #18 <u>Interview:</u> When they say "My girl," they mean it! Friday night, is girls' night out. The sisterhood that extends to peeing (see entry #13), takes on a higher understanding when drunk, i.e., Friend; 'a', takes the right elbow, friend; 'b', takes the left elbow. This allows friend 'c' to pee without unbearable strain on her thigh muscles. The bladder is full after boozing, so peeing takes longer. Her friends also shield her from onlookers, though at this stage of drunkenness, she doesn't care.

♂ #19 Cell phones are a good distraction. Many of the body postures that would otherwise make your peeing obvious are hidden as long as your waist down view is at least obstructed. Fake a call, talk loudly and be demonstrative. (Use hand gestures.) Very effective between parked vehicles.

♂ #20 Cold weather offers a multitude of options. It's the coat. This enabled me to walk along a moderately busy street, passing an occupied patrol car while peeing into the sidewalk grate using my open coat for cover.

    Now! Ticket that Barney Fyfe.

♂ #21 Little pedestrian clearance, bend at the waist to a 90° angle keeping knees straight. Spread feet wide and amble around in one spot pretending to look for something on the ground. Pee while ambling.

♂ #22 When drinking coffee, tea, soda, or whatever. Set the container on a mailbox. Stand between the mailbox and a parked vehicle. Look pensive and pee. (The double boxes are best.)

♂ #23 Got a little pedestrian clearance? Stop at the giant planter or the tiny tree and pee fast. Guess what? No splash!

♂ #24 Take any reasonable cover and wave to your imaginary friend, who's a half block away. Pee on a wall or something to limit splash.

♂ #25 Same cover, look up and point. Pee fast, this doesn't distract for long.

♂ #26 Same cover. Talk to that imaginary friend on your cell phone. While peeing, use a lot of shrugs and gestures.

♂ #27 Duck behind a pole. You need to be skinny for this one.

♀ #28 <u>Observation</u>: Women's worst public peeing problem is that it can take too long. One Saturday night I observed two women behind parked cars squatting almost to a seated position. Peeing rivers! Their dates were double parked standing in the street. The women were on the sidewalk, as was I. I saw them from a distance so I slowed to allow them time. I'd walked 100 feet or so before one of them finished. Still with 60 to 70 feet between us I slowly continued. By the time I walked past, the woman was still peeing. Fortunately for her, West 19th street doesn't have much foot traffic at 1 am on a cold, January night. Of course, me being the gentleman, I pretended not to notice. psst, Nice Booty.

♂ #29 If it's really freezing, anytime past dusk, anywhere, just open your coat and pee. The whole town's a urinal.

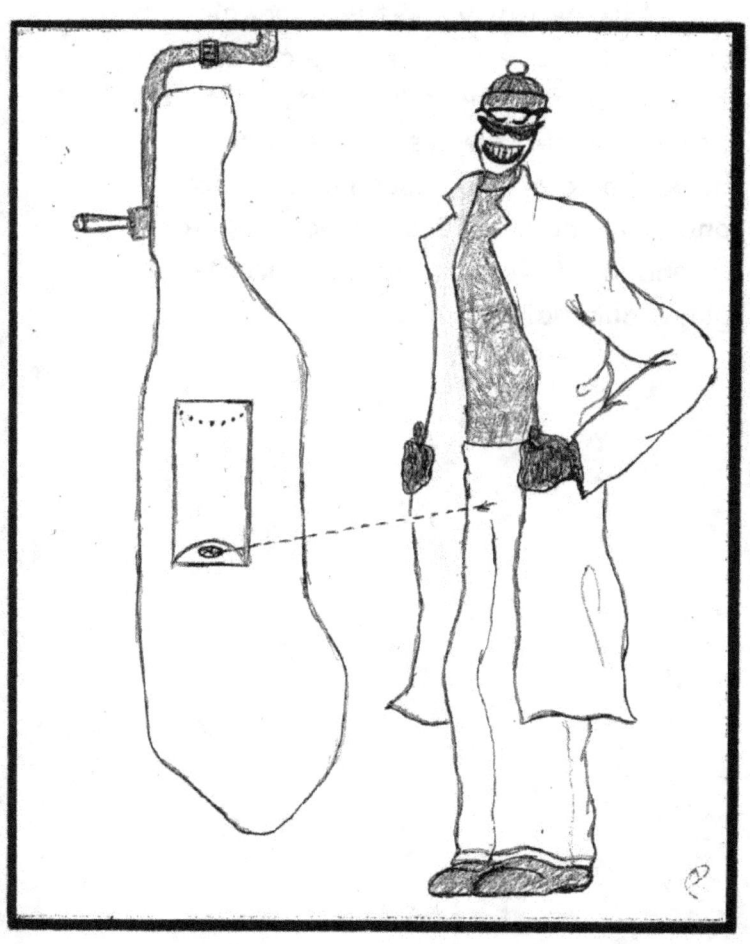

♂ #30 Not only are fewer people out when it's cold, everyone goes about their business paying little attention to others. And it always seems to be dark. Look into an unoccupied window, open your coat wide, so as not to pee on it, and let it flow harmlessly down the glass, eliminating splash.

♂ #31 Fortunately, New York doesn't often get blizzards that leave mountains of snow. However, it happens. When it does no motion. If you have to go out, problem. If you have to pee while out, no problem. You can pee right in the middle of the street. It's also the only place you can walk. The snow absorbs the splash. Once the clean up begins, there are temporary snow hills all over town to duck behind and pee.

<u>Caution</u>: DON'T EAT YELLOW SNOW!

♂ #32 A,B,C's, of good technique. Coats or jackets offer cover but require slightly more attention. (Panel B/C).

- A. Aim toward a wall whenever possible. The pee flows down without splashing.
- B. Open jacket, holding the outside flap (street side), to hide that you're peeing.
- C. Hold your inside flap back so you don't pee on it.
- D. Space your feet and sway your aim to miss your shoes.
- E. Always minimize splash.

♂ #33 Since this is about commuting, we must include one subway riding solution. Walk between two cars of a moving train, hang on and pee.
<u>Caution</u>: Don't' do this while the train is in the station.

This is the only subway entry, and I don't even want to know any other ways.

♂♀ #34 The subway stations that have exit only stairwells are perfect. These stations are indicated by red, or half-red, globes at the stairwell. The globes are color coded like traffic lights; Green = go and Red = stop. Make sure the train isn't in the station. Slip down the stairs, and let it flow. Works for women as well, as I've observed.

♂♀ #35 Scaffolds offer good cover, as well as nooks & crannies for peeing. Avoid the places that others have discovered. As you pee, it activates dry urine of others. Within 3 seconds of your leak it stinks like piss so heavily, it seems as though the odor will contaminate your clothes. Scaffolds offer adequate cover for hiding in plain view.

♂ #36 Construction sights are good. Not only do they have scaffolding, they also have trailers for crew bosses and large containers for dumping. Both structures are parked at the curb, hiding you from traffic. Day or night, stop and pee. Construction workers pay you no attention.

Not recommended for women.

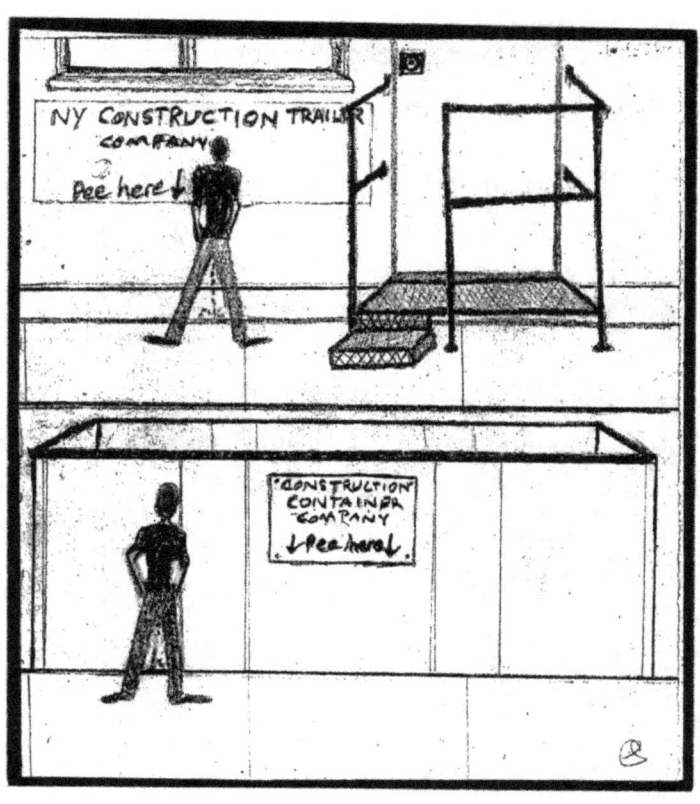

♂　　#37 Dumpsters are good for a number of reasons.

1. They're put out at night.
2. They're placed close to buildings.
3. They're big.

With a little pedestrian clearance, get close to a wall or beside the dumpster and pee on it to limit splash. Still be careful of your shoes. Look into the dumpster if necessary. Embarrassing but effective.

♀ #38 <u>Interview / Observation (Demo)</u>: Women can be so smooth. Especially those bohemian types who wear earthy clothes, with long billowy skirts. Kneel deeply (like knee bends), with your back to a wall. Place your carry bag in front of one knee and search through it. The skirt offers full coverage, but be sure the front isn't touching the ground. The pee flows between your feet forward. Best results if you're at a sidewalk grate. Of course nights are best.

♀ #39 <u>Observation</u>: Saturday night, 1am, W. 19th St. between 6th & 7th avenue. (What is it about this street?) While waiting for a friend, I noticed a car parked 30 feet or so from where I sat. Two women were inside. The passenger got out acting strangely.

      She got back inside and opened the front and rear door of that side. She was hidden well enough by the doors so that the whole time she was peeing , they both looked at me with that " we know that you know" grins, and giggled. I couldn't see her pants down, the squat, nothing. I could see the pee splashing into the street. After she peed "the Hudson," they closed the doors and drove away laughing.

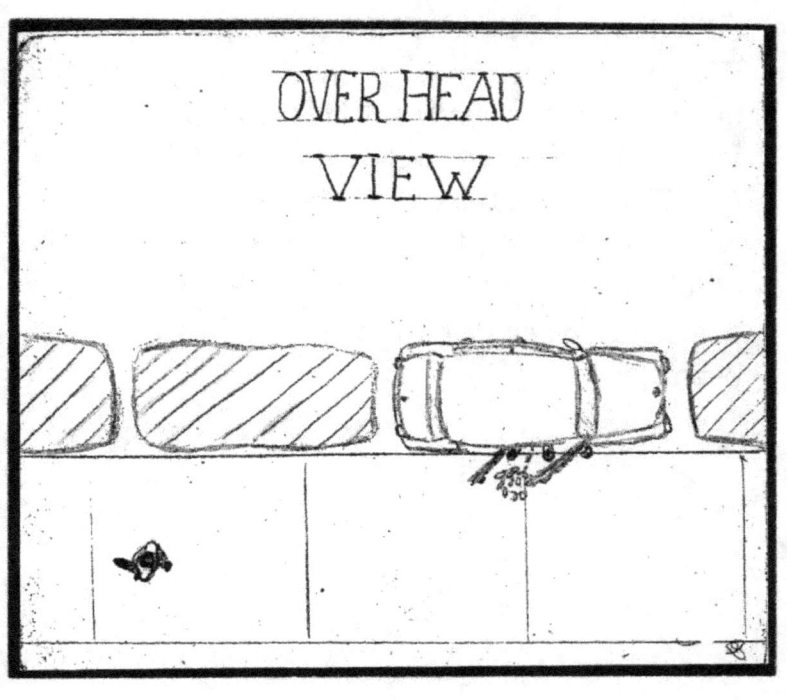

♂♀ #40 Except for the entries that require a coat, runners can apply any method. The attire makes it easier. Still we must have one runner's entry. Try to run thru or near parks. The air is better, the ground is softer, there is less traffic, and so on (see entries # 11 & # 12.) Go to a bench. Sit half on half off. (see entry #14.), make minor adjustments to your gear, and you can pee while you appear to take a breather.

So next time you're on your way to wherever and that "the closer you get the more you gotta go" thing happens, don't rush to get there and then dash into the bathroom with seconds to spare. Be a man, pee in the street.

R. Tempus

Next Book By Ray Tempus

Last One Gone Turn The Lights Out

January 2007